Distant Thunder

Distant Thunder

Poetry by Charles Huckelbury

Cover Design by Liz Calka & Carla Mavaddat
Text Design by Sonia Tabriz & Saba Tabriz

BleakHouse Publishing
2012

BleakHouse Publishing
NEC Box 67
New England College
Henniker, New Hampshire 03242
www.BleakHousePublishing.com

Robert Johnson - Editor
Sonia Tabriz - Managing Editor
Liz Calka - Art Director
Rachel Cupelo - Marketing Director
Shirin Karimi - Senior Creative Consultant

Carla Mavaddat - Assistant Art Director
Susan Nagelsen & Charles Huckelbury - Senior Consulting Editors

Erin George, Negeen Karimi, Emma Lydon,
Chris Miller, Meryl Nolan, Zoé Orfanos, Courtney Scantling
& Saba Tabriz - Consulting Editors

Copyright © 2012 by Charles Huckelbury

All rights reserved. No part of this book shall be reproduced or transmitted in any form or by any means, electronic, mechanical, magnetic, photographic including photocopying, recording or by any information storage and retrieval system, without prior written permission of the publisher. No patent liability is assumed with respect to the use of the information contained herein. Although every precaution has been taken in the preparation of this book, the publisher and author assume no responsibility for errors or omissions. Neither is any liability assumed for damages resulting from the use of the information contained herein.

ISBN-13: 978-0-9797065-9-2
ISBN-10: 0-9797065-9-9

Printed in the United States of America

For Susan, of course.

Table of Contents

About the Author
About the Designers
Acknowledgments

Distant Thunder --- 1
Needless --- 2
"What Did You Do?" --- 3
Romantic Limitations --- 4
My Fourth Anniversary --- 5
The Now Of IT All --- 6
December 3, 2007 --- 7
Postlapsarian Workout --- 8
Gauntlet --- 9
Homage To Seurat --- 10
Omar's Error --- 11
When She Was Four --- 12
Revelation --- 13
Under The Bodhi Tree --- 14
Re Balzac --- 15
Consistency --- 16
Sunday Morning --- 17
January Sophistries --- 18
Dead --- 19
Apathy --- 20
First Light --- 21
Focus --- 22
The Game --- 23
A Gourmand Rejoices --- 25
In The Universe Of Parole --- 26
A Late Dinner --- 27
Perspective --- 28
A Small Case Of Schadenfreude --- 29
The First Noble Truth --- 30
Rest --- 31
Understanding Victor Hassine --- 32
Tailspin --- 33
The Verdict --- 34
Fairy Tale --- 36
Manifest Destiny --- 37
Alteration, Perhaps --- 38
Amnesiac --- 39
Going --- 40
Manchild --- 42

Cruising --- 43
Secret Friend --- 44
And So It Goes --- 46
An Excess Of Epidermis --- 47
No Peace --- 48
A Badder Bladder --- 49
Epilogue --- 50
Nap --- 51
Sun Maid --- 52
Differences --- 53
Angel Butts --- 55
Learning Curve --- 56
A Logical Explanation For The Virulence of H1N1 --- 57
Nocturne --- 58
Salvation --- 59
Snow --- 60
Kill Zone --- 61
Structural Defects --- 62
Ozymandias Redux --- 63
Pelagius Lives --- 64
Pleistocene Memories, Holocene Regrets --- 65
Ovine Observations --- 66
Instant Replay --- 67
Act V --- 68
Close To Henniker --- 69
On Thanksgiving --- 71
Encore --- 72
For Susan --- 73
Façade --- 74
Morning Run --- 75
19 January --- 76
The Minimalist --- 77
Inside The Outside --- 78
Burning Tiger --- 79
Routinely Dead --- 81
Some Final Thoughts On A Final Day --- 82
Dislocation --- 83
Phobia --- 84
Sonnet To Solace --- 85

About the Author

CHARLES HUCKELBURY is a member of the Poetry Society of New Hampshire. His fiction has won Pen America Prizes. He is the Associate Editor of the *Journal of Prisoners on Prison*. *Distant Thunder* is his second book of poetry.

About the Designers

LIZ CALKA is an award-winning photographer and designer, and recently graduated from American University. She is the Art Director of BleakHouse Publishing. Calka has always been drawn to the arts and strongly believes in the power of visuals. She has designed multiple book and magazine covers for BleakHouse Publishing, and she also created the BleakHouse Publishing website.

CARLA MAVADDAT is an undergraduate student at McGill University with a passion for photography and design. She is originally from Montreal, Canada, but she grew up in Washington, DC. Mavaddat is interested in human rights and social justice, and advocates on behalf of the impoverished.

SONIA TABRIZ is a merit scholar and J.D. candidate at The George Washington University Law School. She is the Managing Editor of BleakHouse Publishing and has designed the text for several books and journals. Tabriz is best known for her award-winning works of fiction, including poetry and short stories, as well as her legal commentaries. She co-edited and contributed to *Lethal Rejection: Stories on Crime and Punishment* (Carolina Academic Press, 2009) and *Life Without Parole: Living and Dying in Prison Today* (Oxford University Press 5th Ed., 2011).

SABA TABRIZ is an honors student at American University and serves as a Consulting Editor for BleakHouse Publishing. She is particularly captivated by the human anatomy as understood by science, as well as abstract notions of life, death, and everything in between. Tabriz's written work is featured in BleakHouse Review and she designs the text for *Tacenda Literary Magazine*.

Acknowledgments

Thanks to Sonia Tabriz at BleakHouse Publishing for her patience in formatting the book and, again, to Robert Johnson for making it all happen. Working with you is always a pleasure. A special thanks to my sons Eric and Adam, who continue to provide inspiration for poems where one would hardly expect it. I am so proud of you both. I couldn't let this book go to print without paying tribute to the source of everything worthy on these pages, my wife, Susan. What a long strange trip it's been, one I would not have missed for anything.

Distant Thunder

For six days I've stared at the same sheet of paper
waiting for the poems to come, poems about
gold and jewels and treasure:

---

holding hands and walking into town to get a cone of
pistachio, smoothing supple skin at two in the morning,
reading Emily Dickinson aloud, lying face up in the rain
and not giving a damn about our clothes or the neighbors,

---

sitting on the floor with Kiki and Rocco climbing all over me,
their sweet puppy breath in my face,
raking the garden and pulling weeds to get it ready
for another year, watching your butt
while you climb the stairs ahead of me,

---

listening to roadhouse music and dancing like nobody's
looking, standing at the door when the kids come home for
Christmas, and running late again for work because
you flashed me after breakfast.

But I can write poems only about what I know, and
I don't know enough about gold and jewels and treasure,
which is why I'm still sitting in front of the same page
and waiting.

Needless

When you travel alone
you avoid
hateful lovers
friendly enemies
predatory prey
religious atheists
everyone who isn't anyone
and you get to die
like you dream –
unbroken.

"What Did You Do?"

A high school reunion, a sister, and
a few memories from the old neighborhood
brought a voice I hadn't heard in fifty years.

She talked about her family and the house
I knew too well, the patio out back and the
bushes that hid the brook and us. She

---

talked about her husband, someone who had
played football a year behind me, and I lied
when I said I remembered him.

She was going to buy the books and journals
with my poems, essays, and stories in them and
read everything because she

---

wanted to know what happened to that kid
from down the block who played kick the can
on soft summer nights and who

---

crept down to her house to whisper through the
screen and listen to Buddy Holly whenever she
had a sleepover with five other girls.

We tried to recover a half-century's
interruption until the second letter came
with the big question, and

---

when I answered it, I knew it would be the
last time either of us wrote. That kid who
played under the street lights and

---

made pajama-clad girls giggle grew up
to become someone neither of us recognizes.

Romantic Limitations

I can't write poems like Wordsworth's because I
can't sit by a river a few miles above Tintern Abbey
for inspiration.

I can't write poems like Coleridge's because I don't have
a lime tree bower to shield me from the elements and
prying eyes.

I can't write poems like Keats's because the only
Grecian urns I've ever seen were in pictures or
illustrations in textbooks.

I can't write poems like Shelley's because I
don't believe the West Wind will pay any attention
when I fall on the thorns of life and bleed.

But I can write poems like Gray's because I can imagine
sitting in a country cemetery and contemplating
some dead people, most of whom are still breathing.

My Fourth Anniversary

Four years married, and I
feel like I am just sitting
down to a banquet,
with my wife but
---
her sons are grown
my mother is dead and
my dad can't walk.

I am just sitting down while
the table is being cleared.

The Now Of IT All

I have a cup of
green tea
by my left hand,
pen and paper
by my right.
My dog is snoring
softly at my feet.
The Christians are
all at church, and
the football games
have ended.
I read poems about a
mountain recluse and
think of my wife
eighteen miles and
two lifetimes
away.

December 3, 2007

It's 8 degrees and
the wind moans
at the bars
trying to get in.

The guy below me
tosses and moans
in his sleep
trying to get out.

Postlapsarian Workout

At 5:30 I'm running hundred-yard laps
        alone in the snow.
The guard in the darkened tower
        sits like God
and watches. I know how
        Adam felt
after he learned to miss Eve.

Gauntlet

At 2:00 a.m. my life is a
variation on the
Bayeux Tapestry –
                castles besieged
                dragons slain
                damsels rescued
                conqueror proclaimed.
At sunrise, the warp and weft
collapse into a
moth-eaten remnant –
                a solitary rebel
                on barren plain
                sparring with
                phantoms.

Homage To Seurat

Prison is like a
Sunday afternoon on the Isle of La Grande Jatte.
From a distance, it looks real, as if
it has substance, but up close you discover
that it's actually nothing but a scam,
a scattering of meaningless dots that just
happen to bump into each other
and form human shapes that aren't
really human at all once you learn to look closely.

Omar's Error

A Persian
proverb
promises
that when
it gets dark
you can see
the stars. But
what if someone
puts a hood
over your head?
Or buries you
beneath
brick and steel?
Or stabs you
in the eyes
with an ice pick?

When She Was Four

Her dad knocked her out on Christmas Eve then wrapped
a thin blanket around her thinner body before carrying her
to a park and tossing her down beside the merry-go-round.

They found her the next morning dusted with snow
inside the circle of footprints she made when
she woke up alone and scared in the dark
---
wondering where she was and why she was
before lying back down with her tears
frozen to her face.

Composed after reading about an actual case in Philadelphia.

Revelation

He ran the first time he faced
other men with other knives,
leaving his friend to die
between overflowing toilets in the prison's gym.

He tried to explain how the fear
shut down his brain's
loyalty center and pumped
adrenaline straight to his feet but

---

the rest of his crew were apex predators
who knew nothing about fear and
believed nothing but
payback.

He asked them for another chance, and
when they came for him, as he knew they must,
he showed them he could do better.
He didn't run that last time.

Under The Bodhi Tree

The book promised a mind as calm as
        the moon shining on a tranquil lake, so
I followed the instructions on
        posture and breathing until I could

---

see a white light, but
        I should have read a little more
before I began because the next chapter
        talked about the real me beneath the

---

conscious mind, a place where I would be more
        loving and compassionate and forgiving,
where I would learn to ignore insults and even
        assaults by my fellow travelers, which

---

naturally made me toss the book back on the
        shelf where I got it before I learned
to love and forgive all the people who persist
        in being a pain in my ass.

Re Balzac

Life is not as ugly
        as a kitchen; it's
more like
        a bathroom but
smells worse, and if you're
        going to accomplish
anything, you have to
        get your hands dirty.
Just remember to wash them
        when you're done.

Consistency

When you've
got a number
on your chest and
on your butt,
---
and you can't remember
the last time
someone called you
by your first name,
---
you can count on
at least one person
a day trying to make your
life miserable.

Sunday Morning

I could see my breath as soon as I opened one eye, and
my feet felt like blocks of ice as I tried to yank
the stubborn blankets up over me. With the other eye
crusted shut, I sat up and discovered that
I was on top of the bedspread . . . naked.

I swung my legs off the bed, pulled my other eye open.
It took me a minute to find crumpled jeans on the floor.
I stepped into the frozen legs,
grabbed a dirty sweatshirt from a chair,
and staggered into the living room, where powdery snow
covered the floor and dusted most of the furniture.

The shotgun was propped in the corner, four empty
shells in a semicircle on the carpet – penitents
worshipping a vengeful god.

Through the open front door, my car's surviving headlight
emitted a faint accusing glow from two feet away, then
slowly faded, like life draining from a hospice patient's eye.

The sun streaming through the back glass made a
spider's web of the cracks in the windshield.

I pushed the door shut as pieces began
to assemble themselves,
bringing part of a laugh on the side of my mouth
that didn't have stitches.

January Sophistries

When I'm running in the dark
at minus 19 and three layers
aren't enough –

When the yard lights begin to
twinkle like distant stars as
my tears freeze –

When the others are still asleep, with
full bellies, warm and comfortable
under their blankets –

When hunger is a constant friend and
the canteen has no oatmeal or
anything else that I eat –

When the mail room destroys all the
anniversary cards my wife
sent me –

When my paper disappears because
some asshole can't afford fifty cents
to read the comics –

When I forget again how to say
No to people who want a part
of me –

When I think how unprepared
and unaware
those strangers are –

When I laugh through the pain
that keeps me warm at night
and serves as a constant
reminder of who and where
and not like them,
my catechism is complete.

Dead

On the day they find out I'm
dead, people who hate me will
                celebrate,
---
but I hope the people who love me
will think about better days before
                I went to prison
and died there.

And I hope, too, that the ones
mourning outnumber the ones
laughing.

Maybe they'll read something I
wrote, something that made them
laugh or cry.

Maybe they'll call Susan and tell her
how sorry they were that we never
had the life we planned.

She'll wait until they hang up before
crying and maybe calling me every
worthless bastard in the book
---
for leaving her like that, just as her
book came out and she got famous
and the world was ours.

Apathy

It's 3:00
and I'm awake
                again
self-excluded
from the others
self-deluded by my
successes
at being what
the rest hate
---
someone who
won't talk
won't listen
won't care
who they are
or
what they do
---
when they
aren't reading
my poems.

First Light

Aurora
Eos
Goddess of the morning
Homer's rosy fingers
over Troy

Call it what you will,
dawn behind the walls
doesn't do anything but
begin just another
day you have to do.

Focus

Pen and paper
I have and
green tea and a
black Lab
for company
while I make
my poems.

I also have
football games and
"Desperate Housewives"
on nineteen TV's
to stop me
from making
my poems.

The Game

We get bananas once a month and
bagels once in forever. This morning
we had both, so the cops tried to
---
stuff 200 guys into tables built to
hold 120. When I got my tray,
with the banana and bagels and
---
peanut butter on the side, I looked
around for a place to sit, but the only
open seats were next to the rats and perverts.

I could have stood against the wall and
tried to eat or just circled the room in a
holding pattern, but that would have
---
meant letting the cops win. Instead, I
took a breath, and then threw it all away,
forcing my hand not to grab the banana
---
at the last minute and stuff into my
pocket to take back to my cell
and eat later. I heard the guys
---
in the dish room on the other side
of the window celebrate when
they saw my tray come in the slot.

I walked past the cops who had
watched me throw out my breakfast,
the same ones who jammed me
---
in there with all those other guys
trying to eat their chow standing up,
but they didn't look at me on the way out.

I was stronger because I wouldn't play the
game, but it's still hard not to roll over when
your belly's screaming at your brain
---
to stop the silly shit and forget about
the cops and the other guys and
eat the banana and the bagels.

A Gourmand Rejoices

The grilled chicken was tossed together in a
        sodden pile along with fresh broccoli and
buttered noodles. A plastic fork lay across it all,
        its handle flecked with saliva and food.

Tupperware scraps from a nothing fancy table
        where unchained people ate every night,
but when the shop foreman asked the
        old con if he wanted any of it,
---
he didn't give a damn that it was cold or
        half eaten or that it might have sawdust
mixed with it or that his boss might have
        spit in it as a joke.

All that mattered to the old con was that it wasn't
        fried baloney and kidney beans and better than
the last Christmas dinner he had eaten on the street
        at McDonald's when Big Macs were fifty cents.

In The Universe Of Parole

Only
two seasons –
hope and
despair –
with a
five year
period of
oscillation.

A Late Dinner

The snow on the wire
will trick you into taking
a bite but beneath the
marshmallow the razors
will cut your mouth and
stab your tongue
and hold you until
the tower guard shoots
you in the head
and changes the snow from
vanilla to strawberry.

Perspective

It was a good fight he tells me
putting two fingers four inches

apart on his forehead
to show me how wide the cut was.

He knocked him down and stomped
him he tells me

miming the motion with
leg and foot.

I think he broke his jaw
in two places he tells me

hitting himself on the
point of his chin.

It was a good fight but
left me wondering:

what makes a bad one?

A Small Case Of Schadenfreude

At 5:30 in the morning I watched Randy
yodel in the toilet, then stagger back to
his cell without flushing. Maybe he got
sick thinking about the little girl he raped,
or maybe the ghosts of all the people he
told on came back to haunt him. Then

I shook my head. His conscience has been
on life support from birth, so he must be
dope sick again. I looked at his
belly spilling over his underwear and
the spindly legs struggling to handle the
load. And loved it.

I should be a bigger and better person.
I should be able to find that thread that
unites us in our common humanity.
But not this morning, not with him.

Maybe tomorrow I'll get in touch with
my better angels. Maybe I'll say a prayer
for him instead of celebrating his pain.
Maybe I'll wake up on the Cote d'Azur
with my wife in a string bikini beside me.

The First Noble Truth

Freedom is when you
stop giving a fuck and
---
dare the rednecks to do
their worst because
---
you are tired sick and tired
of the calluses on your knees.

Freedom is when you
will kneel no longer.

Rest

No poet's gentle slide into a good night
my father's death was a gasping struggle
among the jungle of tubes and wires
that sustained him and connected him
and emptied him until he was left
the detritus of a chemical factory
slowly closing its bankrupt doors and
bidding farewell to its CEO,
the last half of my DNA, crowding memories
ghostly coasting around the fringes
of what perhaps never was
and will not be again.

Understanding Victor Hassine

Susan wrote her book
because no one knew,
and then
---
she flew to London
to present a paper because
no one listened,
---
which was published in a
journal that no one
read after
---
the Supreme Court said the states could start
killing people again because
no one cared.

Victor saved them the trouble and killed himself
because twenty-six years was enough.

Tailspin

This morning I watched a jet's
contrail etch a salmon
line across a bruised sky and
wondered again who was on the
flight and where they
were going.

And I wondered if they knew
about the steel and concrete
passing below them and
the men in identical uniforms
who might be staring up at
them from five miles away.

I wondered if they knew
how lucky they were to be
on the way to wherever they
wanted, to be traveling with
someone they love, even to be
complaining about the airline's food.

Probably not. Most people who don't
have to make count don't know they're
free, don't know that the lousy
transcontinental chicken would be a
five-star meal for the people buried
beneath their wings.

The line began to fade after a few minutes,
finally dissipating until I could hardly
tell it had ever been there. After wondering and
wishing until it all disappeared over the walls,
I went back to my seat on the ground
and continued to wait.

The Verdict

Every two weeks I made the long walk from
my cell to Michael's to cut his hair. His trial lasted
long enough for six haircuts.

I couldn't take scissors into his section, but it
didn't matter to him. He wanted it cut down close,
the way he wore it when he killed the cop who was
chasing him.

He was a Red Sox fan so we naturally talked
about baseball until they had no chance at going
back to the World Series. When the weather changed,
we talked about football because he was a Patriots fan, too.
The last time I cut his hair before the verdict,
he told me that Brady sucked but he thought the Pats
would go all the way.

I wanted to grab his shirt and shake him and tell him that
the state was trying to kill him, that football and baseball
don't mean shit when you're dead, but I don't think it
would have done any good. His eyes were younger than
his body, and children know nothing of death.

So instead I packed up my clippers while the guard counted
everything and then gave me a pat search.
Michael held out his cuffed hands, and we bumped fists.

"Thanks," he said. "I'll get you when I get out of there."
"Right," I said and moved toward the slider
when the guard pointed.

Three days later, his max cell became his death row cell.
The jury said he didn't show any remorse and had
committed robberies and assaults. They wanted someone to
hang him or shoot poison into his veins.
They said he knew what he was doing that night in the alley.

A week after that, I went back to cut his hair again. The Patriots were playing Miami, and he hoped he would get his TV in time for the playoffs.

Fairy Tale

A solitary house just where the road
bent out of sight peeped through
the branches in a homerun away.

Trimmed in yellows and blues, it
resurrected the Grimms and invited me in
to explore gingerbread smells and tastes.

And the witch?
She didn't scare me nearly as much
as the bars I was looking through.

Manifest Destiny

Death beckons most from a
polar landscape: cold and dark,
where guttering candles cry over
a grief-crusted coffin.

But He waves to me from Aruba,
drink in hand, warm breeze in his face,
and a forty-eight-footer parked
at the quay.

Alteration, Perhaps

I have a sense of closing, of ending, of a
final performance of some as yet undisclosed drama that
is about to play out for a small audience.

I feel change of the permanent variety, but I
can't trust those feelings that deserted me when
my mother died unacknowledged.

The alternative is logic, which often fails me
in this most illogical of places. Then there are
the voodoo assurances of
---

three witches who want me to bury things when
the moon is dark. But how would I explain to a
guard why I'm digging a hole
---

to bury a bottle of piss and hair and a piece of cloth when I'm
supposed to be in my cell during
count at shift change?

In the end, there is once again the vast nothing,
the inability to do anything but wait for it.
Whatever *IT* is.

Amnesiac

When you finish the first ten, you still want
the things you see on TV,
the cars, the jewelry, and the girls,
mostly the girls.

By the time you finish twenty,
you've learned that you can live
without the cars, the jewelry, and the girls,
mostly the girls.

At the end of thirty, you can't remember
why you wanted the cars, the jewelry, or the girls,
mostly the girls.
And you don't care.

Going

I woke sitting on a friendless bench in the dark, a bent
metal post prostrate on the ground next to me.
My feet rested on a rusting sign that read
WAIT.

Ten feet away, obdurate weeds split the asphalt
of a two-lane road while their cousins groped
blindly up the bench's leprous legs.

A melancholy wind blew traces of sand across my face. I
brushed at it and looked at the blood on my fingers,
scratched the ache in the center of my chest
through the hole that obliterated Jerry Garcia's face.

I checked the road again and heard it,
keeping my face turned forward,
trying to discover which direction the sound came from.
I sang "Magic Bus" and thought about Rosa Parks
and where I would sit.

Then I saw it, headlights out, bouncing and jouncing
across the open field in front of me, dull aluminum skin
pitted and cracked, windshield spider-webbed and
the wheels churning a black wake. The brakes hissed once
when it stopped in front of me, waiting,
huffing its patient predator breath.

The doors opened with a sigh,
and I stared at the empty driver's chair
before pushing myself off the bench and putting one foot
on the stairs, then another
until I could see the length of the bus.
A hint of music, something Teutonic, Wagner maybe
or Beethoven, rolled over the single empty bench that
guarded the immaculate interior. A printed card was taped
to its black plastic: RESERVED.

The engine revved impatiently.
The door flapped eagerly behind me.
I took a last look at the solitary, scabrous seat,
the dirt, the weeds, the empty night under
an indifferent moon.

I got on board.

Manchild

Today I celebrate
six decades of wandering this
Earth, bringing equal parts
love and hate.

Seven hundred twenty months of
constantly searching for
knowledge,
---
often unencumbered
by any sense of what to do
with it once I found it.

Twenty-one thousand, nine hundred
days of trying to figure out who I am
and why

I'm here to write poems
about loving and hating,
searching and knowing,
turning sixty
---
but still acting twenty-five.

Cruising

At a certain age
life becomes a trip
in the rearview mirror
a long road behind and
a short one in front
a world of memories
instead of events
until the car runs
out of gas or
if we're lucky
crashes before the
parts begin to break.

Secret Friend

After grabbing my sweats at 4:30 while
my wife sleeps, I pick up my sneakers and
follow my shadow out the door to the
bathroom to do all the clean-me stuff.
I dance a busted-knee boogie past the
all night flicker of Eric's television before
---

running warm water over my hands
so I can close them, then it's a cold
splash in the face and a quick look to
make sure it's the same eyes staring
back at me.

My shoulders snap when I try to brush my teeth,
so I prop up one elbow and go from there.
Then the left ankle buckles when I try to pick up the
toothpaste cap, but a quick hand on the sink
saves me from disaster. The shower comes last
leaving high and low parts untouched.

I get to the kitchen just as NPR softly
welcomes the day to keep me company while
I stretch. My hamstrings are reinforced concrete,
but I convince them to move a couple of inches. I
rotate my head and hear the Rice Krispies go off
in my neck as the shock runs down to my fingertips

Fifteen minutes later, my joints and muscles
are as good as they're going to get. I bend and
try to reach the floor, feeling the scar
over my spine lengthen. The sweat drips on the
floor in front of my face, the puddle mocking
my reflection. I'm nearly ready.

I move to the counter to eat five pills
before heading outside to run. The first three
steps remind me that my body has been coping with

my madness for 62 years and that this will be just
another day in the same old routine. I'm back
in five minutes, limping into reality.

I settle for instant oatmeal and green tea and sit down
at the breakfast table. When I lean back against the wall,
hips, knees, and shoulders join in a symphony
that builds in brass and timpani before slowly fading
in a vibrato of strings.

I close my eyes and hold the tea with both hands
while the movie in my head begins to loop,
old football games, stupid fights, and heavy bench presses
drift in and out, ache alternating with pride, while
I finally summon my body to stillness. For what
will be the only time this day, there is no pain.

And So It Goes

Sixty years of
wearing out my body
and still I don't stop. Even if
the old man's
wrinkled skin didn't
threaten to shatter my
illusions, I would
run
        and lift
                and strain
because it's what I do,
and the pain
that keeps me company
at night is a
trifle when
I think about what would happen
if I ever stopped.

An Excess Of Epidermis

When I needed more skin
to accommodate my bench press,
I couldn't find it anywhere, so my
perpetually pregnant chest and shoulders
sprouted stretch marks that still look like Amtrak routes.

Since Social Security started coming monthly
and my shoulders have finally quit on me,
I don't need the extra skin, but now
I've got enough of the damned stuff left over
to cover two sofas and a recliner.

Published in *Poet's Touchstone*, Fall 2009.

No Peace

Through the window I could see
a mix of snow and rain that fought
against a toasty bed that pulled like
a tide at the full moon. My watch
read 4:30 when I rolled over
for thirty more minutes.

But then I heard
the voice from long ago
that always shames me, warns me,
and gets me out of my comfort zone.

"When you're cold and tired and hungry,
and the weather's bad and you want to stay
in bed, there's another guy out there who's
also cold and tired and hungry and wants
to stay in bed, only he's out running
when you aren't, and when you meet him,
it won't be pretty."

Thirty minutes later I was passing dark
windows and locked doors, warm bodies
tucked in with smiles on their faces and
other bodies next to them, dreaming about
coffee and eggs and bagels and
wool sweaters and dry boots.

Rain and sweat dripped from my nose and my breath
puffed white in front of me. I wanted to slow down
but then I heard the voice again:

"Be ready, stay ready, or you'll be like them."

A Badder Bladder

When I was twenty, an all nighter
Meant gallons of coffee and
cramming for midterms or finals.

Now that I'm sixty, an all nighter
means I don't have to get up to
use the bathroom.

Epilogue

My knees are shot
my back is out
and like as not
I'm just about

---

to close this show
and get on down
to where folks go
when lost or found

---

or if they then
have just been fired
or often when
they're so damned tired

---

of all the lies
and all the pain
to plan a rest
and rue no gain.

Nap

It happens only during the day,
on a cool October afternoon
when the house is quiet and
---
the blanket feels like it should be
up to your chin and the window
open to a hint of woodsmoke.

When you find that special place,
the one that drains the tension out of you
from the valve at the base of your spine,
---
then you discover that a dreamless peace
is the best relief possible and death
isn't such a daunting master after all.

Sun Maid

The small red box lay in the
blackening snow
crushed into a rhombus by someone's careless
boot print on the young girl's face,
obliterating the tray of
ripe green grapes she was carrying
and knocking her bonnet askew.

Once I would have picked up that box,
brushed away the dirt and sand, and tried
to smooth the creases from her painted smile.
But her face and arms, even
the subtle swell of her breasts
under the loose blouse,
are no longer
real to me
---

as they once were when I would
open my school lunch and look for the
raisins first and talk to the smiling face
and create stories about helping her
pick the grapes and then setting them on
the windowsill of a small house with
painted shutters so they would dry quickly.

Differences

One January, when the wind-chill was minus fifty,
I sent a friend in Florida a weather clipping from the paper.
He asked me how we lived up here and what we did
when it was that cold.

He didn't know how easily I can find that special place in
bed, the one that infuses body and brain
with a delicious lethargy that tugs at legs and arms
beneath extra blankets piled like woolen a ziggurat
on top of me and no eye-stabbing sun
when I wake to an undisturbed earth with knee-deep snow
muffling the rest of the world's rage and disappointment.

He couldn't guess how many books I read during the winter
with my dog at my feet and a cup of green tea near my hand,
while the wind moans its solemn oratorio around the
doors and windows and rattles down the chimney.

He's never smelled the wood smoke ushering in
crystalline skies so blue and hard
that jets trail diamond-etched contrails
on their way south with cargoes of the timid and tame,
fleeing a nor'easter or arctic express.

His geography stops at the Southeastern Conference,
ignoring Ivy football and midterms
at the best colleges in the country,
shadowed by an ice-skating Christmas and carols that
aren't trapped in malls full of shoppers in shorts and
tee shirts and sandals and black socks.

He doesn't know anyone who will pause
and speak to you on the street
when it's forty degrees below freezing or stop on their way
to watch their youngest daughter's starring role
in the school play
if someone is in the crosswalk.

His imagination can't conjure this country, where it's dark at both four o'clocks and water spilled in November doesn't melt until March.

Angel Butts

In one of Botticelli's paintings, a cherub's
gossamer wrap falls away to show a tiny butt,
---
which must have been a mistake because
angels don't sit or shit and therefore
---
don't need butts, or maybe they do and
nobody told us because if angels sit and shit, that
---
means God must sit and shit too, since
we're all made in his image, but I can't see

God perched on the can working the Sunday
crossword because he would know all the answers.

Learning Curve

I discovered Bohr's theory of the atom
in a tenth-grade chemistry class, and
its elegance and mathematical precision
fascinated me, at least until

I discovered quantum theory's
electron clouds and the impossibility
of measuring both position and
momentum reliably, but soon

I discovered that both theories
were able to describe what became
obvious as I grew older and got
to know people better:

---

we are mostly empty space.

A Logical Explanation For The Virulence Of H1N1

The flu is now on the hunt for your house
or conceivably still searching for mine,
thus the only sure way to be safe is
to hide so it can't uncover or find
---
where we are and begin to infuse us
with the virus that murders unfairly.
Beware the beast can often confuse us
when fully dressed or clothed only barely.

After all it remains easy to see why
this flu strain of flu has gotten so big:
it's Swine Flu and its targets are we,
unregenerate male chauvinist pigs.

Nocturne

Night is the better teacher,
revealing and concealing, gliding
over skin that feels as if the
top layer had been sanded away,
leaving the nerves exposed to an
elevated threshold of
diversity and perversity before
the sun casts its sanctimonious
eye on the result.

Salvation

Finally the quiet,
the dark, the cold
the solitude,
the way heaven would
look and sound
if it were real.

Snow

She told me how her father
would wake her every year
when the first snow fell
early in the morning. Together
they would watch the outside
world turn white with
his arm around her shoulder.

She told me he died when
she was still in college and how
every year after that when the
first flake fell before dawn it
broke her heart to think about him
lying beneath the snow that he had
loved so much.

And now she too lies cold beside him
leaving only one of us to watch the
early snow cover the grass above them.

Kill Zone

Failures are
sly bastards,
lying in ambush
when you think
you've gotten
them, like that
forgotten glob
of jelly on the
edge of the table
you put your hand
in the next day.

Structural Defects

Why would an omnipotent God,
        a god who had all the engineering skills
and all the tools he needed to create a
        perfect being in his own image,
---

decide to build a face upside down
        with the nose over the mouth so that
every winter one of his nasty little
        rhinoviruses –
---

which God also designed to have a little
extra fun with his invention –
---

makes its home in the nose and causes
        a river of snot to pour from both nostrils
the most convenient place for it to stop
        will be the first open spot?

Because before he got that far, God also invented
Bernoulli's principle and hollandaise sauce.

Ozymandias Redux

The desert is the best place to see what
      we will leave behind
      when we're finally gone:

---

all the books and music, all the guns and tanks,
      everything that makes us
      who we are, confirming

---

what we've done. There, too, will be the residue of
      our hopes and dreams,
      faded and bleached to ghosts

---

as the sun expands to incinerate
      everything until only
      the suffering remains.

Pelagius Lives

Contrary to what
many people tell you,
faith is not enough.
If you want something,
you can't wait around and
trust someone else
to make it happen for you.

You have to become
a heretic and actually
do the work yourself because
there's nothing out there but
an indifferent universe ready
to put a foot in your butt.

If you're waiting for
divine intervention,
that bus left the station
the day you were born.

Pleistocene Memories, Holocene Regrets

Forty years ago I treated the world
        as my private sea,
swimming sharklike through
people and places, never causing a
        ripple to announce my presence until
I was ready to feed, then moving on
        to susceptible latitudes, leaving
the rest to pick up the broken pieces
        and wonder who or what was among them.

But now the anonymity that once
        served my purpose and buoyed my pride is
turned to stone that carries me ever deeper
        and threatens to drown me in a faceless,
nameless sea with no trace I was ever
        here and with no chance for redemption.

Ovine Observations

Before Darwin, I wolf-eyed people in the cities and towns
I passed, waiting for the lame to limp or the sick to stumble.
They were sheep, going about their timid lives, working and
shopping and taking care of the kids – and oblivious.

Evolution finally overtook me when I woke up and wanted
to be like them, to be a sheep and do all those sheep things
I ridiculed before I outgrew my claws and teeth. Now I
work, shop, take care of the kids with the rest of the flock.

And I know someone else is driving those same highways,
passing through those same towns and seeing the
same things I saw. And I wonder if he's watching
and waiting for me to limp or stumble.

Instant Replay

You came running down the driveway
waving the newspaper in your hand and
yelling because I hadn't told you that I had
made all-city that senior year.

You threw your arms around my neck before
I had a chance to tell you that I didn't know
about the selection until just then, but once
I told you, you hugged me all the way inside

the house and said that you had called Dad
at work and told him as soon as you had seen
the paper. He was on his way home with a
big smile and a special meal from Leo's Deli

to celebrate. The all-city pick got me
a football scholarship, and you and Dad never
missed a game, no matter how far you had to
go to be there for kickoff.

Forty-five years have come and gone, and so have you,
but I'll always remember you as that young mom
who ran down the driveway to tell her
only son how proud she was of him.

Act V

When you came in from yard work that Sunday and sat
in your recliner for the last time, maybe you felt your heart
begin to stumble and had time to think
So this is what it feels like
before you slipped away.

You never panicked when healing the rest of us –
skinned knees, fractured loves, and a child's
determined disappointment – so you probably just shrugged,
as if death were a movie you could take or leave,
depending on the actors.

Two years later we talk about the lessons you taught us
such as the summer night a fifth-grade boy learned that
his PTA mom could outrun him with ease, or how you
insisted that you loved the scrawny back of the chicken we
had for Sunday lunch and the skin and gristle we left behind.

Your chair is in the same place, and Breezy still bounces
on the ottoman to look for you
and the special treats you gave her,
then runs to your bedroom to bark her anticipation. But
the empty space sucks us into despair of a heart now silent
that beat only for the people you loved.

Close To Henniker

Two winters after my mother died, when the
snow and ice covered everything and made
the forage look and feel like a Popsicle, the
deer she always fed came back.

The first winter they stayed away, as if they knew
she wouldn't be there to spread the feed and
warn them about straying too far into the woods
during hunting season. They always paid attention because
most were mothers with kids, and they knew
another mom wouldn't lie to them.

But they came back, new moms with new babies,
bunched behind the house and all the hardwoods and
perennials, so thick in the spring you can
barely walk from the rear door to the fence
where they now stand waiting. They look at the
blank windows with wet, hopeful eyes, pausing
every now and then to sniff or lick one of the fawns,
antsy in the way of all children to eat and then
play but smart enough to stay close to mom when
the guns are out.

My mother won't be there again for them
to spread the sweet corn and talk softly before
going back inside so those other mothers will come
close enough to feed warily, ears up and reflexes taut
for any sign of danger. Now they will have to rely
on a stranger to carry on the tradition that my mother
carefully passed along to her family and friends,
just as the deer have passed along the same
tradition to theirs.

The corn is on the frozen ground in the same place, and
Linda will try to soothe the fears and coax the deer closer.
Maybe they'll listen and come in, but maybe they
won't recognize either the voice or the form and stay
beyond the tree line with their gnawing hunger.

It might take a year or two or even three
before they are comfortable again,
and if they come back next December,
the empty space where she stood with her bucket
will confirm that my mother is gone. It won't be the same,
even when the food is there.
For the deer or for me.

On Thanksgiving

I miss her.

Me too.

I talk to her all the time
but usually in the car so people
won't think I'm crazy.

I talk to her at night
after everyone else is asleep
and can't hear me cry.

It isn't fair.

I know.

We can't forget her.

She won't let us.

Encore

When Death finally closed my father's show after
a run of eighty-three years, it brought down the

curtain to a standing ovation, the audience
acknowledging what we had all seen –

a bravura performance by a superstar, in which
the rest of us were fortunate understudies.

For Susan

I watched you grow, learning the ways but
trapped by
        people dictating who you were and
what you should be,
        people censuring your choices and
ignoring your courage in making them,
        people who never read your stories
even though they were in them.

They laughed each time you fell, mystified
when you got back up, wiped away the
disappointment, and tried again with
I-told-you-so echoing echoing echoing
against your solitary yes.

Your first story told me about you and them. Your
teacher drove home alone through a defiant night,
hands beating time on the steering wheel before
the trip segued into more people and more images, and
I saw how good you would be.

When your stories came alive
in magazines and journals and books,
the tour took you across the country and to Canada,
and then to London
where international minds stood and clapped
for what you read to them.
You grew and stretched and became and still

---

the others did not read, did not know, did not care.
They were ruts in the road, passed over with barely a bump
until they gradually faded in the rearview mirror while
your teacher sang along with Stevie Nicks
as she drove into the sunrise.

Façade

You laughed when my mother told you
how she had cried all day when
I left for college.

You smiled when you thought about how
empty the house would be and the shower
all yours any time you wanted.

You grinned when you packed up the video games
and anticipated mornings with no television –
just you, your coffee, and NPR.

You sighed at the promise of getting the paper
whole and not having to hear how the Niners
had done the previous day.

You celebrated a future two thousand miles away:
a new office, a new neighborhood, a new life,
a promise to call weekly.

Then you cried where Eric couldn't see you as he pulled out
of the driveway while you waved and held the puppies
to keep them from running after him.

Morning Run

Bending on the edge of
our bed
I tighten the laces
thirty minutes before
the sun.

You roll toward me and
prop on one elbow, your
other hand on my back. You
---
ask if I have to go. When
I turn, you move and
the sheet falls away easily.

Bending on the edge of
our bed
I loosen the laces
twenty-eight minutes before
the sun.

19 January

It rained just enough to melt
the top two inches of snow,
turning the exposed layer into a
dirty glacier, three degrees hard
even at noon,

---

hard like these winters, hard
like the people who endure them
before turning their faces into
the April sun to thaw,

---

like peonies responding
to their diurnal rhythm.

The Minimalist

On our worst days, when we're tempted to curse
fate and whine that the world hasn't given
---
us a chance, we forget that the world doesn't
owe us a chance; it recognizes no obligation
---
to any living thing. At sunrise each morning,
when the coral sky is shot through with
---
magenta streaks, and the hush is so
profound even the geese pause
---
to take a look, that's all we're entitled to.
And perhaps all we need.

Published in *Northern New England Review*, 2002.

Inside The Outside

While you pile more wood on the fire
and move closer to its warmth,
out here beyond your circle of light
in the cold and dark
I can smell your food and
hear your songs.

I watch your children play, all
your touching and feeling,
your doing. You forget that I'm
here, always here, and you
trust the fire to keep you safe.
But it destroys your night vision
---

which means you can't see me even
though I can see you from my darkness
while I wait for the rain that will
put out your fire and teach you
about the fertile shadows
where we both will then live.

Burning Tiger

Hearing our favorite morning
voices with their glib morning patter
sparks coffee images adorning
---
sports pages and things that matter
to most of us in our frantic urge
to worship heroes. A flatter
---
earth offers rank and praise to purge
the famous in the firmament
of the real and recite the dirge
---
that transforms clay to permanent
status, invoking for the men
fault-proof armor and talents meant
---
to woo the women, all number ten.
Then to Facebook we came, eager
to match voice with stellar face, when
---
out leapt a mix so meager
with pedestrian human mugs
that belonged on no big leaguer
---
and produced only agonized shrugs.
Idols are become wisps of smoke,
invalid as a hangman's hugs,
---
fit only for a Leno night joke.
So we were consistently wrong
and now like the rest seek to poke
---
a hole in the best singer's song
because his veins run red like ours.
Why the rage? It was we all along
---

who swore the PGA tours
grew players with no morning breath
and whose homes needed no sewers.

No use to blame a public death
on any man who abdicates;
we still have no churlish King George
---

or anyone else who dictates
who we love or lovingly hate.
But still our star ingratiates
---

with looks and style we yet call fate,
and so the rudeness of the fall
hurts us more than his hapless mate.

Routinely Dead

One man paces the perimeter of the exercise pen,
green pajamas fluttering in a gelid wind.
He absently kicks a basketball in his path
but disregards the portable goal
only a foot higher than his head.

He ignores the snow that dusts him like a sugar cookie. The
eyes look nowhere but a step ahead of his feet as if
breaking trail in a rain forest or searching
for something he lost.

Cozened and cosseted by psychotropic friends, he
takes 31 seconds to make a lap, walking steadier
than he will in another month.

Soon another joins him, then another until a harvest
of eviscerated souls forms a shuffling parade under the
newly installed lights that let the walkers, the talkers, and
the stalkers come out at night.

But it's the same view for all of them, sun or moon,
and all the same to them, because it's always dark
in that private place behind their eyes.

Some Final Thoughts On A Final Day

Two days before Thanksgiving, the greedy
carnivores surrounded Steve's bed to watch
him die, some thankful that they weren't needy
enough to help him walk and maybe catch

---

the blood and bone coming from the shower.
Others were thankful that the bags were now
in the sterile bin where their old power
could no longer affront them. No matter how

---

hard they tried to erase the sights and sounds
of Steve's laughter as he planned the tiny tots'
toys, they recalled his face on their daily rounds
and rued their own lives for the haves and nots.

Word reached the herbivores beyond the walls,
but they were unthankful because they must
search for a new piñata, one that calls
for mercy, instead of Steve who roundly cursed

---

them all and refused to burst and overtly spill
his secrets, which prompted the sticks to land
harder and harder, seeking blood until
they gasped, wheezed, admitted, "This is a man."

After twenty-one years Steve escape from
tactical friendships and professional
indifference, winking the selfsame aplomb
as we went not to the confessional.

Dislocation

The distance
between us
is the thing,
the thing that's
a thousand
times two miles
as the crow
flies, if the
crow could find
its goddamn
way to hell
or Phoenix.

Phobia

When I was six, I woke from a nightmare
crying and convinced that an unidentified
monster lay in wait for me behind
our refrigerator. My father came to my bedside,
listened to my fears, and then took me by the hand.

He led me gently into the kitchen, a reassuring arm
around my trembling shoulder. Leaving the lights out,
he went first to the dark place where my fear lurked and
then held out his hand to me until I slowly walked to his side
and discovered only the compressor's low hum,
not the creature's sinister breathing.

I learned that night
not to fear the dark but more important,
not to fear what or who might be in the dark.
My father's loving care and patience helped
mold me into someone who could survive
the violent environment where even then
he must have suspected I was headed.

For nearly forty years, I have lived and worked and played
among the most dangerous predators, shrugging off threats
and wounds and periodic attempts to kill me. I have
feared nothing since vanquishing the kitchen beast.

Now my father lies petrified, barely coherent and raging
against the tubes and wires that keep him connected
like a perverse umbilical to a world he no longer knows.
He screams for release and begs me to shoot him
in the head and give him peace.

But I fear life without him in it, the dissolution of my
last bond. I cannot lift the weapon and put it against
his clammy temple. I am weak and frightened,
and I am sorry for the betrayal.

Sonnet To Solace

At a low frequency, a woman lights
a cigarette and waits with a shotgun
behind the door to spill the hate-filled blood
of the man who shook her like a rag doll.

At a raunchy higher frequency, a
poker-playing drunk ends a losing night
by pulling a pistol and shooting his
erstwhile best friend right between his blue eyes.

Country on one side, rock on the other,
rural or urban, gunpowder and lead
and Saturday night specials are still the
preferred arbiters. And in the middle,
---
a weak signal from a tiny station
just offers "Ode to Joy" as anodyne.

www.ingramcontent.com/pod-product-compliance
Lightning Source LLC
Chambersburg PA
CBHW072016290426
44109CB00018B/2252